Somehow
Helen Calcutt

VERVE
POETRY PRESS
BIRMINGHAM

PUBLISHED BY VERVE POETRY PRESS
https://vervepoetrypress.com
mail@vervepoetrypress.com

The right of Helen Calcutt to be identified as author of this work has been
asserted in accordance with section 77 of the Copyright, Designs and
Patents Act 1988.

FIRST PUBLISHED SEP 2020

Printed and bound in the UK
by Positive Print, Birmingham

ISBN: 978-1-912565-42-9

Cover Art Credit: Katherine Sheers

CONTENTS

for Matthew

Somehow

Now my brother has died

the flowers have opened. The sound of a
river is moving in my head,
the startled flowers –
Or is it blood? heart? – their ephemeral
mouths opening and closing. How dare they
grant me this steady life. The strength of it.
I want a stillness, still I
go on, like the soul of a river, living loud
with other rivers, longing for murdered roses and
the resurrection of a hanging
clock.
How dare this life
make me want the things I'd die to
love, but river-bound, never could.

Something terrible happened

the phone rang
and when I answered

it you'd killed
yourself, and that was the start

of you being dead.
All I could think about

was hurting someone
I loved. I hurled myself

into the glowing
garden,

I tore at the leaves
then the light. I told

my daughter not
to cry (though I

should have kissed her eyes)
and for days I couldn't

speak. Dry thorns, dirt
on my cheeks, I looked

for signs of rain,
sudden clouds,

anything
that held your

death
in the clement weather.

Light

For days now,
light

has been walking in through
the window. For days,
the leaves have followed it.

When I look one way
they flock the sun.
Their foldings flicker like innate

conversation. For days
I have wanted the light
to be just light. But the way she carries her body

is tipsy thin
and the trees are too:
they lift up their hair, and weep

tipsy song.
And they are leaning
and talking

and making everything
about the circumstances of the light –
the way she folds and clutters

and tussles and mutters
and makes everything bright in the room—
it feels so *crude*.

All the aching corners
I wanted to be hard
have softened to the tune of her touch

in her brightest moments,
as I've cowered and cried
or gone crazy on the bed

light
      has thrown light
              and pulled the sobbing up over my head...

and they have said

grief

is a family of birds
thrown from the nest,

that light in this capacity
must be some coincidence.

He isn't in the room.
He didn't come.

My hands aren't wings
and the roof doesn't burn.

Waving, or drowning?

After Stevie Smith

When he came alive, you leant in,
a red flower to his whisper.
What he said, was darkness
from the bud of the spine, so you turned away.

You still remember the sound.
If you close your eyes, you see his mouth
white, soft,
an embryonic sack, opening and closing.

Nothing like the confusion
of water to make you think
something's alive. Was that a hand there
in the swell of the screen

lifting or waving? A child or a man,
floating, drowning?
You leant in one more time, but had gone too far
to make sense of it.
Now you see, you expected it.

A conversation with my daughter about my brother's suicide

She is awake.

The moon is bright and the clouds have parted.
The trees are painted trees, living a still life.

She tells me my brother is in the moon.
I've bathed her, given her milk
and as I fold the sheets from her knees

to her lap,
she asks me how he died.
He was very sad, I say
and she seems to understand.

She rubs the milk away from her lips with her hands
as if the moon had kissed her,
and then asks why.

I try to explain.
Sadness can make you very tired,
it can make you want to sleep,

it can make you want to close your eyes on everything.
Her hands are leaves
resting on the bedcovers.

She asks me if I miss him
and when I say I do,
she asks me again, how he died

if the sadness of missing him
will make me die.

I hold her then,
I accept
the weight of her. I can feel her widening like the stillness of a tree –

my child, coming into a still life...

Then we talk about the moon being
the shape of an egg, upside down.
Watch branches touch on drifting clouds

and agree – we want to see everything.

Wonderful

Over the years they've climbed
to the very lip of the sash,
her fingerprints.
And where she's knelt, bowing
upwards, a golden reed
the marks have scattered
a constellation of effort;
the hours, days, weeks,
of learning how to grow.
She loops her fingers
around my thumb,
and my heart unlocks. You see,
it's that she's touching
me, and whenever someone
touches me (especially
her) I want to cry.
I want to tell her
I love her. But instead
I say, *mommy's sad
today*. She slips
from the bed
to the floor, walks
to her little stool:
opens the window.

Found

Words taken from coroner's post mortem report, October 2017

She found him in the dark at the bottom
of the stairs. Body of a male, hanging
by ligature. The mark was deep, 1cm
but no scar.
She had to cut the suspension point
with scissors
the ligature,
in circumference, 47cm.
Impression is of someone
with moderate anxiety.
Who appeared at times of domestic distress,
ideated suicide, but denied
intent.
Larynx, trachea, bronchi,   *normal*
mouth, pharynx, oesophagus,   *unremarkable,*
history of anxiety since 2006
prescribed citalopram
20mg
20mg...
No ligature   *received,*
There is nothing
significant about
the deceased.

Bath Time

Knowing I have to leave,

knowing this

is the only thing that keeps me here,
ornament and subject to your keen advances,
your careful taps.

You want to see if I'm still alive.
I bloom when our daughter touches me,
but when you...

my skin draws a pallid glaze
and I want to hold
and hold

another innocence of feeling.
I don't want to be loved in any other way.
I'll keep on making the pure things

the sweet-blood, growing things.
I'll be still, like pottery
and let the green stems grow,

the vessel and charm
you want to nibble on, and suck.
Lie smooth and round,

depressed in the bath.
Let the water come over me
like fakery in sex,

and like all those other times, I'll
lie back, and listen for hope in the rain.
Stare hard, like those trees

with their hair thrown forwards.
I've learned to feel their downward ache.
I know what kind of life that is,

sustaining a fall.
Barely alive barely breathing.

City birds

You hardly notice at first.
One bird, then another
singing across languid knots
of trees, gilt with blossom.

It grows with the emptiness of streets,
the are lamps muted, blind, yet listening,
and even that woman in the park
fucking her man

hears the call,
drawn like a thread through
the needle of their throats.
The city bird's song.

Always at this time.
The bus stops are full
of people waiting to be taken to their gates,
eyes behind glass, and hands in their pockets

swaying with the dusk that halos their jackets.
I pray for their angelic shuffling.
My bus arrives, but I don't
get on. I want to stare at my feet while the birds

thrill me, and think of that free woman having sex–
all that pleasure she'll have among the ferns and ash,
I want to know
want to know

how hard and how
beautiful the collapse of their bodies
when it's done.
Does her hold her, limp

or does she draw away over him, and stand
while the birds
tremble sweetly over his finishing?
Does she see the bus glide up

over the hill? Just as I've
watched it go, wondering
if that lovely woman has cum between her legs,
and what it feels like, with these first stars

and the dusk in its silence
the loaming loveliness, this
fall-away quietness.
I want to lie down here, sleep.

I want a stranger to part the wings of my coat
to lift these hips,
and let the good grace of sadness
really enter me.

Finally, the birds might stop.
I might sing in their place.
I might weep. I might bleed.
I might feel *something*.

Sing dove

She knows your body can gaze through
the matter of a person
like music through dust.
She knows you can lie there
or climb there,   and sing dove.
She's watched you think about
stabbing your own hands
with a knife, wondering if the tree out there will bleed
in Autumn, if its branches
will lower, if your body
will tighten, when you loop the bind
and give your weight to it.
She has watched your brother die
by his own hand
many times. That's why
she's here
banging the fences at night. Going
round and round the entrance
to your house. Raking
hands over the floor.
Giving blood to the stone—
so you might hear her.

A mountain that is your grief you can't utter

I remember the night I saw one, as I crossed the bridge.
Its long wings slipped into twilight over my head
and it landed, grey amongst shadows
with the river running, as it does here, fast
and dark: like dirty coins amongst the glitter.

I wanted to follow it, though I was going home to a house of light—
I stared hard, the stars,
wouldn't come forward

and I looked a long time
from the mouth of the bridge,   feeling for a mountain,
with the dark bearing down, like a wing.

I saw the sloping
                            bones

        of the heron,

    I felt desire.

And then a longing to bend   just so

with my head on my chest
and a long mouth

and my heart,

beating just inches above the iron bed of water,

to know it intimately, like a friend.

Rope

He counts the length with his thumb.
How many lives?
Like the shadow
of a red tree the moon
eclipses, how suddenly will he
disappear?
And by 'how many'
I mean, how many will grieve?
When he falls backwards
into that dark stair, and the roof
smiles down, like a mother,
will there be branches closing
round? Will something sweet on the air
lift him, make it quick, take
his body pale and priestly to God?
Or will he struggle
like a fish on the end
of his hook? Will his baby son
finding the bed is cold
go looking for daddy? Will
his son's father's father
wake, with a racing heart
to the sound of geese
turning their hearts overhead?
Will the length of time
counting the minutes it takes
to die

deter him from dying? Will the journey
from his bed, to that dark stair
hold him back, just enough,
hearing some
blowing resistance, and stop—
Or is this all a dream
I want to make
into poetry? Did he even count
the length of rope, thinking
of us, maybe, as he ran the length
between fingers and thumb, not
counting, but knowing. Was this
one of those rare, yet
common moments? As when swans
burst out of the sky,
catching fire,
burning from the world as they hit water
that we don't even see?

Brother blowing

somewhere, I am
somewhere between
sleeping and waking,

        the whole blowing silk of our tent

     lifting and inflating
          needy as a lung.

Midnight perhaps, or not long after.
The moon has disappeared, the black
wind cries in the leaves;

the whole sky's a blowy saint;
  the sound of trees.

My child lies asleep in the corner,
  unaware.

A storm
     is moving into our room, conductive as a hand;
  I fold my blanket over her ears, her precious head.

All around,
  the sky that lives out there
is moving in here;

our bed space swings,
the tassels knock   as coast clouds

        sent in far over the dark
                unrest the body of our gentle room.

They'd said it would come.   It's both sad and beautiful
to watch the light blow, watch it go with the air
                so easy,
    then return again as easily...

I lie, I

breathe
    within thin walls
                astounded.

    I imagine

jellyfish brains smashed over a rock—
that   *we are the only light*

    while our tenting soul
flaps to climb

                high

                        as

                                high

oh, are we

anchored

just right?

And it's then

you drop flight
hollowed bird,

my brother blowing.

   You smile, as you enter the room,
you make breathing noises

you set down
        the two ends of your being
like cloth

you set down
        the two ends of your being
like the wings of a dove—

   you wrap the cloak of your exposure
around my eyes   strangely warm

and when the tentpoles shake   I can feel you've come

feel that death isn't dark
        that the dead aren't bright

they just come this way when you need their light –

and I truly see you, my God. I truly feel you here.
It's so *good*   to be like this
fearful, but alive

                    alive

                    and so very, very

                                                far

                                                            from
where you died

            oh my brother

        how you're blowing

                    in my ears and eyes.

Grief is like a miracle

like opening your mouth for water, and finding rain.
You stand for days outside the body of a silent church.
Snow touches the stillness of the windows and
you long for their acceptance, a few tears.
You tell yourself the door isn't closed:
it's open and weeping.   Like the orange rose
that never bloomed all Spring
then one day in Autumn   opened atriums of colour.
Now all the roses gather and the door
is open-armed. People think I'm strange
touching my lips to the wood, but
ice is thawing to love inside my body:
I don't know how else to show my gratitude.

Wind

for Matthew

You must have folded the sky
back in on itself, thrown caution
to the wind. Those faintest of cries. The kind
a dog hears
slipped out like a star
and tipped a cold shadow over the moon.
The weight of that drop
you felt and heard,
heard and felt,
for miles, over that distance,
and into the distance,
and under the milestone of your heart.
Like the wind,
it was faltering a long time.
You held your breath
when she barked, and when she cried
you dragged what love
you thought would find
a way through the bullying wind,
out of the storm.
How burdening the blight of this –
the bloody effort. Now the days stretch
with the long years of corn
you laboured under; blowing a wild,
sorry lament
under the broken sun—

and the wind,
she comes so breathless now
to blow and break apart all her sons.

The blossom tree

I imagine sometimes   the blossom tree unlabouring its roots
walking towards me with soft eyes   saying
it can't remember whether it is human or a tree   I say
you are lilac   and in a way this seems sad   that it can't remember
whether it is human or a tree   but I am amazed—
it lifts the tender   heavy-groan of its roots   one weighted foot
in front of the other   and with a leaf-sigh
lowers cross-legged to sit in front of me

its stillness and stirrings touch the eye
of my window   it looks into my circumstance   and tells me
I will be okay duly   in a voice like a river   though deep and
tunnelled somewhere dark with other rivers

it hangs over me   a body of rain
wiped over with light – it has come to me soft and smelling
sensual   I know that its manner of swaying suggests prayer
but I don't want to lay down my head   the thoughts I have are of him
coming to me
or going from me   under a canopy
of sun-washed trees   in a suit or jeans   climbing
as you would a stair   as you would a heavy climb
unto the gentle rocking of a high   noose

the blossom tree   hears this   nods   its hair shakes snow life-affirming
and asks me   if I really believe he is dead?
and when I say *yes*   in that lucid moment   that dreamic
crystal   binary moment
something heavy will press against the glass   and make light
 – and the blossom tree   will exhale to rise
those cords   its branches   from hollow to end
extending like Christ's limbs   lifting away with the sun gasping—

and all around the sky will take the blossom in abundance
the sky our mother   the sky our God
and the tree will look up   seeing itself float   and the moment it stands
will be incredible
all risings of pain   all risings of joy   floating like Christ
with his hair on end   and every sinew will crack
as the blossom goes up   and the tree will turn and start to walk
with all this strangeness happening   as if it were the very making of its
own mind

and I will blink as it goes away
bleary from the sun and air   with all the suddenness that moved
the blossom   raiding my sight like tears   and a kind voice

and I shan't know who I am or what has happened

ABOUT THE AUTHOR

Helen Calcutt's poetry and critical writing has appeared in the Guardian, the Huffington Post, the Brooklyn Review, Unbound, Poetry Scotland, Wild Court, Envoi, The London Magazine and others. She is the editor and creator of Anthology Eighty-Four which was a Sabotage Best Anthology short-listed title, and a Poetry Wales Book of the Year, and raised money for CALM's prevent male suicide campaign.

BY THE SAME AUTHOR

as author:
Unabler Mother (V.Press, 2018)
Sudden Rainfall (Perdika, 2014)

as editor:
Eighty Four: Poems on male suicide, vulnerability, grief and hope
(Verve Poetry Press, 2019)

ACKNOWLEDGEMENTS

Thank you to the editors of the journals in which some of these poems first appeared: *Southbank Poetry, Irisi Magazine, The Cardiff Review, Poetry Wales, Wild Court, Ink Sweat and Tears*. My deepest gratitude to Arts Council England, Peter Stones, and to Zoë Brigley Thompson for her wonderful editorial insights. And thank you to the wonderful Stuart Bartholomew for his dedication and support.

ABOUT VERVE POETRY PRESS

Verve Poetry Press is a fairly new and already award-winning press focussing hard on meeting a need in Birmingham - a need for the vibrant poetry scene here in Brum to find a way to present itself to the poetry world via publication. Co-founded by Stuart Bartholomew and Amerah Saleh, it is publishing poets from all corners of the city - poets that represent the city's varied and energetic qualities and will communicate its many poetic stories.

Added to this is a colourful pamphlet series featuring poets who have previously performed at our sister festival - and a poetry show series which captures the magic of longer poetry performance pieces by poets such as Polarbear and Matt Abbott.

Like the festival, we will strive to think about poetry in inclusive ways and embrace the multiplicity of approaches towards this glorious art.

In 2019 the press was voted Most Innovative Publisher at the Saboteur Awards, and won the Publisher's Award for Poetry Pamphlets at the Michael Marks Awards.

www.vervepoetrypress.com
@VervePoetryPres
mail@vervepoetrypress.com